How To Use This Study Guide

This five-lesson study guide corresponds to *"How To Have Peace of Mind in Troubled Times" With Rick Renner* (Renner TV). Each lesson in this study guide covers a topic that is addressed during the program series, with questions and references supplied to draw you deeper into your own private study of the Scriptures on this subject.

To derive the most benefit from this study guide, consider the following:

First, watch or listen to the program prior to working through the corresponding lesson in this guide. (Programs can also be viewed at **renner.org** by clicking on the Media/Archives links or on our Renner Ministries YouTube channel.)

Second, take the time to look up the scriptures included in each lesson. Prayerfully consider their application to your own life.

Third, use a journal or notebook to make note of your answers to each lesson's Study Questions and Practical Application challenges.

Fourth, invest specific time in prayer and in the Word of God to consult with the Holy Spirit. Write down the scriptures or insights He reveals to you.

Finally, take action! Whatever the Lord tells you to do according to His Word, do it.

For added insights on this subject, it is recommended that you obtain Rick's book *My Peace-Filled Day: A Sparkling Gems from the Greek Guided Devotional Journey*. You may also select from Rick's other available resources by placing your order at **renner.org** or by calling 1-800-742-5593.

TOPIC

Possess a Trouble-Free Heart

SCRIPTURES

1. **Luke 21:26** — Men's hearts failing them for fear, and for looking after those things which are coming on the earth....

2. **John 14:27** — Peace I leave with you, my peace I give unto you: not as the world giveth, give I unto you. Let not your heart be troubled, neither let it be afraid.

3. **2 Timothy 1:7** (*NKJV*) — For God has not given us a spirit of fear, but of power and of love, and of a sound mind.

GREEK WORDS

1. "peace"— εἰρήνη (*eirene*): depicts the cessation of war, an end of conflict, a time of rebuilding and reconstruction after war has ceased, a time when distractions are removed, a time of prosperity, or the rule of order in the place of chaos; a calm, inner stability that results in the ability to conduct oneself peacefully even in the midst of circumstances that would normally be traumatic or upsetting; the Greek equivalent for the Hebrew word shalom, which expresses the idea of wholeness, completeness, or tranquility in the soul that is unaffected by outward circumstances or pressures

2. "heart"— καρδία (*kardia*): the center or core of your being; emotions

3. "troubled"— ταράσσω (*tarasso*): to stir up; to be unsettled; to feel anxiety; to be inwardly moved and upset; to be tossed back and forth; pictures someone who is upset, tossed, and troubled

4. "afraid"— δειλιάω (*deiliao*): to be cowardly; to live in dread; to shrink backward; to move into retreat; depicts a paralyzing fear that produces a shrinking back or cowardice

5. "sound mind"— σωφρονισμός (*sophronismos*): a compound of σώζω (*sodzo*) and φρήν (*phren*); the word σώζω (*sodzo*) means delivered, healed, saved, and whole; the word φρήν (*phren*) pictures intelligence or the mind and speaks of the inner force that regulates outward behavior; as a compound, it pictures a mind that has been delivered,

rescued, revived, salvaged, and protected and which now is safe and secure; what I call "saved brains"

SYNOPSIS

The five lessons in this study titled *How To Have Peace of Mind in Troubled Times* will focus on the following topics:

- Possess a Trouble-Free Heart
- Let God's Peace Serve as an Umpire for Your Mind and Emotions
- Cast All Your Care Upon the Lord
- Keep the Devil Where He Belongs — Under Your Feet!
- Five Important Steps To Move You From Turmoil to Peace

Clearly, the state of the world is incredibly chaotic, not to mention the challenges you may be facing in your personal life. Yet, in spite of everything that is happening around you, you can have an unshakable peace dominating your life!

The emphasis of this lesson:

To combat the troubles and fears we face, Jesus has gifted us with His supernatural peace. Even when we are surrounded by outward pressures and turbulent circumstances, we can remain calm, cool, and stable inside. Our mind and emotions are saved through Christ.

What You See and Hear in the News Does Affect You

In Luke 21:26, Jesus prophesied about what will be happening in the last of the last days, telling us, "Men's hearts failing them for fear, and for looking after those things which are coming on the earth...." Although there have been many tumultuous seasons in history, what is happening collectively on the earth right now confirms that we are living at the very end of the age, just as Jesus described.

Watching and listening to the news reports about everything going on in the world today can certainly steal your peace. Rick shared how, when he and his family moved to the former Soviet Union in 1991, they did not have access to western television stations for quite some time. Therefore, they were unaware of all the troublesome times people in America were experiencing.

For example, when big hurricanes hit Florida and the southern states, they knew nothing about it. Likewise, when there were terrible riots going on in Los Angeles, a growing polarization between the American people, and an escalating war in the Middle East, they were totally unaware because they didn't have access to western news.

In the absence of regular news updates from the United States, Rick and his family went about their days in the former Soviet Union enjoying life and living peacefully. This demonstrates the powerful effects of what we take in through our eyes and ears and what we allow to fill our minds.

A day came when Rick went to Riga, Latvia, to get funding for the ministry from the only western-based bank in the country at that time. As he sat waiting for his opportunity to speak with the teller, he began to watch the news broadcast playing in the lobby. For the first time in a long time, Rick was made aware of the disturbing situations that were going on back in the states, including the horrific effects of a hurricane that was wiping out southern Florida.

Next on the screen were real-time images of widespread rioting in Los Angeles, which included reports of burglaries and fires across the city as well as the murders of innocent people. This news was quickly followed by on-going coverage of the Persian Gulf War and all the events that were happening in the region.

Once all the top stories were covered, the news anchors hit the rewind button and began retelling all the same stories again. By the time Rick was finally attended to by the bank personnel, he had listened to and watched more bad news than he could stomach. He was so upset by what he saw and heard on the news that he had lost his peace.

Again, this brings us back to what Jesus said in Luke 21:26 about the end of the age: "Men's hearts failing them for fear, and for looking after those things which are coming on the earth...." Indeed, we're living in a time when, if we pay attention to all the events occurring around the world — including what is happening in our own school system, local government, and neighborhood — we can lose our peace. So we need to know how to guard ourselves in order to have peace of mind in troubled times.

All of Us Face Various Forms of Fear at Times

In addition to the chaos and calamities taking place throughout the world, each of us has our own collection of challenges that we face. Rick candidly shared about one major event he went through in 1998 that made him come face to face with the pattern of worry and lack of peace that prevailed in his life.

> When I was growing up, I worried a great deal and lacked peace. In fact, I struggled with worry for many years, but God fully exposed it and helped me put it to rest in 1998.
>
> At that time, we were living in Latvia, a former republic of the Soviet Union, and building a large church in the city of Riga. This would be the first church building to be constructed in the Republic of Latvia in 55 years, an area that had been dominated by the Soviet totalitarian mindset. Making matters worse was the fact that we had many enemies who were against the project.
>
> After doing all that was required, the government gave us permission to launch out and build, but they had one major stipulation: we had to finish the project within two years, and if we didn't, we would lose the building, the land, and everything we had invested in it.
>
> To be clear, the church project was going to cost $4 million, which meant we needed a lot of funds. In those days, very few banks loaned money, and no church could get a loan from a bank, which meant we had to believe for all the cash to come in within the two-year window dictated by the government.
>
> At the same time we were building the church, we were also on television. That in itself was a huge step of faith, as airtime was very expensive. We were also publishing books and sending out copies free of charge to the ends of the earth. We were paying for the printing of those books, as well as the envelopes, the postage, and the salaries of the growing team of employees that were doing the work.
>
> To cover the cost of all the things we were already doing, we needed mountains of money, and now with building the church, we needed an additional $4 million — and it had to be done in

two years. This was the biggest project that God had asked me to do leading up to that moment in my life.

Trying to shoulder the emotional weight of the situation left me in a perpetual state of worry. Money was on my mind all the time, and I found myself 'failing for fear' (*see* Luke 21:26). Night after night, I would roll in bed, first one way and then the other. My wife Denise would hit me and say, 'Rick, would you please lay still?'

'But Denise,' I would say, 'I'm so worried. Where is all this money going to come from?'

'Oh, Rick,' she'd respond, 'Would you just give it to the Lord?'

Now when she would say that it would really irritate me. When the TV stations needed payments for airtime and the contractors needed money to buy materials and continue the work, it wasn't Denise they called — it was *me*.

'It's easy for you to tell me to just give it to the Lord,' I would say to her. 'But no one is calling you for payments. They're calling me.' Needless to say, I lost my peace.

But the truth is that Denise was right. I did need to give the situation to the Lord. Since He was the One who wanted the church to be built in Riga, the Gospel to be broadcast on television, and books to be printed, He would need to pay the bills for it.

God used that trying time in 1998 to help me really plug into John 14:27 and come to the realization that it is not His will for me to worry, fret, or live in a constant state of anxiety. None of those emotions will change a thing. They are all just a waste of time and energy. The same is true for you.

Regardless of what is going on in the world around you, God doesn't want you to worry or be anxious about anything. Instead, He wants you to live in and experience His unshakable peace.

Jesus Has Given You His 'Peace'

As Jesus spent His final moments with His disciples before going to the Cross, He told them many things to encourage and strengthen their faith.

One of the greatest truths He spoke to them — and to *us* — is found in John 14:27, where He says:

> **Peace I leave with you, my peace I give unto you: not as the world giveth, give I unto you. Let not your heart be troubled, neither let it be afraid.**

It is interesting to note that the word "give" in the original Greek language is the word for *a gift*. This tells us that peace is a gift given to us by Jesus. He released it, and it belongs to us. We can confidently lay claim to it by faith.

This brings us to the word "peace," which Jesus uses twice in this one verse. It is a translation of a form of the Greek word *eirene*, and it depicts *the cessation of war* or *an end of conflict*. Thus, if you are in the peace of Jesus, you are no longer at war in your mind and emotions. The conflict has ceased with yourself and with others.

The word *eirene* — translated as "peace" — also signifies *a time of rebuilding and reconstruction after war has ceased*. This means that when you are experiencing the peace of Jesus, you are focused on rebuilding and reconstructing rather than on the problems at hand. That is what peace enables you to do.

This peace (*eirene*) that Jesus gives to you as a gift also describes *a time when distractions are removed, a time of prosperity*, or *the rule of order in the place of chaos*. It is *a calm, inner stability that results in the ability to conduct oneself peacefully even in the midst of circumstances that would normally be traumatic or upsetting*. That doesn't mean upsetting or traumatic circumstances aren't happening. It just means that even if they are happening, you are still able to conduct yourself peacefully in the midst of it.

Moreover, the Greek word *eirene* — translated here as "peace" — is the equivalent of the Hebrew word *shalom*, which expresses the idea of *wholeness, completeness*, or *tranquility in the soul that is unaffected by outward circumstances or pressures*. This means when you're moving in peace, even if you're surrounded by outward pressures and turbulent circumstances, you can be like an island of stability that is unaffected.

The peace of Jesus is meant to dominate you and fill your entire life with *shalom*. It is His personal gift given to you and every single believer.

Don't Let Your Heart Be 'Troubled' or 'Afraid'

After informing us that He has gifted us His supernatural peace, Jesus goes on to say, "…Let not your heart be troubled, neither let it be afraid" (John 14:27). The word for "heart" here is the Greek word *kardia*, and it describes *the center or core of your being* or *the center of human emotions*. Hence, Jesus is telling us, "Don't let the core of your being — your emotions — be troubled."

In this verse, the word "troubled" is a form of the Greek word *tarasso*, which means *to stir up, to be unsettled, to feel anxiety, to be inwardly moved and upset*, or *to be tossed back and forth*. This is a picture of someone who is upset, tossed, and troubled, which describes what Rick experienced when he was worried and anxious about receiving the needed money to build the church in Riga, Latvia, and pay for all the other outreaches they were conducting.

Make no mistake: When your emotions (*kardia*) are stirred up, unsettled, and tossed back and forth (*tarasso*), they will begin to take you downward and open the door to an assortment of negative emotions, all of which will try to pull you into the realm of fear.

That is why Jesus instructed us to not be troubled or afraid (*see* John 14:27). The Greek word Jesus used for "afraid" is from a form of *deiliao*, which means *to be cowardly, to live in dread, to shrink backward*, or *to move into retreat*. It depicts *a paralyzing fear that produces a shrinking back or cowardice*. The use of this word *deiliao* tells us that when a spirit of fear is at work in our life, we want to close the curtains and hide because we are afraid of the things that are going on around us.

Friend, you can't function like that. God has things He needs you to do. You have people you need to take care of and a job you need to accomplish. You don't have time to live in fear and dread or shrink back in retreat. Jesus doesn't want you to be crippled or paralyzed by fear of any kind.

Along With Peace,
God Has Given You a 'Sound Mind'

The apostle Paul addressed this same kind of paralyzing fear in his second letter to his spiritual son Timothy. At the time of its writing, Timothy was facing very difficult times, and his problems were not imaginary. Nero was the emperor of Rome, and he was killing Christians all around him. In the natural, Timothy was afraid that he might be killed next. It was for this reason Paul wrote and told him:

> **For God has not given us a spirit of fear, but of power and of love and of a sound mind.**
> **— 2 Timothy 1:7 (*NKJV*)**

Clearly, God has not given you a spirit of fear. Instead, Jesus said, "*Peace* I leave with you, my *peace* I give unto you…" (John 14:27). So God, through Christ, has given you peace, not fear. Interestingly, the Greek word for "fear" in Second Timothy 1:7 is the same word for "afraid" in John 14:27. It is a form of the word *deiliao*, which means *to be cowardly, to live in dread, to shrink backward*, or *to move into retreat*. It depicts *a paralyzing fear that produces a shrinking back or cowardice.*

The use of this word lets us know that God has not given you a spirit that causes you to shrink backward, move in retreat, or live in dread as a coward about the future or the present. Instead, He has gifted you with a Spirit of power, love, and a *sound mind.*

What is a "sound mind"? In Greek, the words "sound mind" are a transla-tion of the word *sophronismos*, a compound of the words *sodzo* and *phren*. The word *sodzo* means *delivered, healed, saved, and whole.* And the word *phren* pictures *intelligence* or *the mind* and speaks of *the inner force that regulates outward behavior.* When these words are compounded to form *sophronismos*, it pictures *a mind that has been delivered, rescued, revived, salvaged*, and *protected*, and which now is *safe* and *secure.* We could even say that a "sound mind" describes a "saved brain."

A mind that is *un*sound worries about everything — even irrational things that will never take place. It is affected by outward circumstances and traumatic events, causing it to move into submission to and come under the control of a spirit of fear and retreat. But a sound mind is saved — it is a mind that is *delivered*, a mind that is *rescued* and *revived*, a mind that is *salvaged* and free of all those outward pressures and influences and is dominated by Jesus' peace.

When You Are Troubled or Afraid, Run to God's Word and Speak It!

Jesus said that in this life we will have trouble, but that we can be of good cheer because He has overcome the world (*see* John 16:33). The next time you begin to feel your emotions becoming troubled or afraid, run to God's Word!

When you feel unsettled, anxious, or inwardly upset, run to John 14:27, and make it your personal declaration. Say this:

> 'Jesus has left me with and has given me His Peace. He has not called me to be troubled by or afraid of these circumstances and events. He has called me to be dominated by peace, experiencing wholeness, completeness, and tranquility in my soul — totally unaffected by outward circumstances or pressures.'

When you feel afraid and have a desire to shrink backward, retreat, or live paralyzed in dread, run to Second Timothy 1:7, and make it your personal declaration. You can say:

> 'God has not given me a spirit of fear, timidity, or cowardice. Instead, He has given me His Spirit of power, love, and a sound mind. In Christ, my brain and its thought patterns are saved! I choose to push fear away and embrace the sound mind and peace Jesus has given me.'

Declaring God's Word aloud over your life is not an attempt to deny the reality of the difficulty and trauma you may be facing. But the fact is that even if you are in a sea of turmoil, Jesus said, "Peace I leave with you, my peace I give unto you..." (John 14:27).

Again, the word "give" in Greek is the word for *a gift*. Jesus has gifted you with His peace, which removes all distractions and all conflict, and it enables you to respond peacefully even to events that would normally be traumatic or upsetting. It is God's will for you to have peace of mind even in troubled times.

In our next lesson, we are going to see how peace can work like an umpire in your life to regulate and to dominate your mind and your emotions.

STUDY QUESTIONS

**Study to shew thyself approved unto God, a workman that
needeth not to be ashamed, rightly dividing the word of truth.
— 2 Timothy 2:15**

1. When you think about *peace*, what scriptures come to mind that have helped you make it through difficult times? How have they strengthened and encouraged your faith?

2. Take a moment to reread the meaning of the word for "peace" and the word for "sound mind" in this lesson. What new insights is the Holy Spirit showing you about the peace Jesus has released to you? How about the sound mind He has provided?

3. Are you experiencing these gifts in your life? If not, pray and ask the Lord to show you what adjustments you need to make in your life to walk in His peace and experience a sound mind.

PRACTICAL APPLICATION

**But be ye doers of the word, and not hearers only,
deceiving your own selves.
— James 1:22**

1. From where do you get the news of what is happening in the world? Be honest with yourself: What effects are these news sources having on you mentally and emotionally? Is it time for you to make some changes to what you are watching and listening to?

2. Allowing yourself to stay in a state of being troubled, upset, and fearful won't help you. So take Jesus' words in John 14:27 seriously and REFUSE to let your heart be troubled or afraid. Pray and invite the Holy Spirit into your life and situation by praying:

   Lord, I need You. I feel fear creeping in, trying to bring me down. Strengthen me now by the power of Your Spirit not to yield to fear in any form. I choose to receive Your supernatural peace, and I grab hold of these negative emotions and pull them in line with God's Word. I will operate in the Spirit of power, in the Spirit of love, and with the sound mind You have given me. In Your Name I pray, amen!

TOPIC

Let God's Peace Serve as an Umpire for Your Mind and Emotions

SCRIPTURES

1. **Luke 21:26** — Men's hearts failing them for fear, and for looking after those things which are coming on the earth....
2. **Colossians 3:15** — And let the peace of God rule in your hearts....
3. **Colossians 3:16** — Let the word of Christ dwell in you richly....

GREEK WORDS

1. "peace" — εἰρήνη (*eirene*): depicts the cessation of war, an end of conflict, a time of rebuilding and reconstruction after war has ceased, a time when distractions are removed, a time of prosperity, or the rule of order in the place of chaos; a calm, inner stability that results in the ability to conduct oneself peacefully even in the midst of circumstances that would normally be traumatic or upsetting; the Greek equivalent for the Hebrew word shalom, which expresses the idea of wholeness, completeness, or tranquility in the soul that is unaffected by outward circumstances or pressures

2. "rule" — βραβεύω (*brabeuo*): used in ancient times to describe the umpire or referee who moderated and judged the athletic competitions that were so popular in the ancient world

3. "dwell" — ἐνοικέω (*enoikeo*): a compound of ἐν (*en*) and οἰκέω (*oikeo*); the word ἐν (*en*) means in or inside, and the word οἰκέω (*oikeo*) means to live; as a compound, it means to live inside, to dwell inside, or to comfortably take up residency

4. "richly" — πλουσίως (*plousios*): incredible abundance, extreme wealth, enormous affluence, great prosperity, immense riches, magnificent opulence, or extravagant lavishness; pictures one who is filthy, stinking rich

SYNOPSIS

In our first lesson, we examined Jesus' words in John 14:27 where He said, "Peace I leave with you, my peace I give unto you...." We saw that the word "give" in this verse is the Greek word for *a gift*. This tells us that it is God's will for us to receive the gift of His *peace*.

Jesus goes on to say, "...Let not your heart be troubled, neither let it be afraid" (John 14:27). The word "troubled" means *to be upset or unsettled, to feel anxious*, or *to be tossed to and fro*. And the word "afraid" describes *one that is shrinking back, retreating, and so terrified by what he's facing that he becomes paralyzed by a spirit of cowardice.*

It is not God's will for you to be troubled or afraid, which is why Jesus has gifted you with His supernatural peace and a sound mind (*see* 2 Timothy 1:7). Regardless of what you're facing in your finances, your marriage, your family, or at work, you can be dominated by peace even if you feel surrounded by a sea of turmoil.

The emphasis of this lesson:

We are to let the peace of God rule as an umpire in our life. Peace should call all the shots and act as referee in our mind, emotions, and decisions. When we're in peace, we're able to think right, act right, and decide right. This supernatural peace is inseparably linked to letting God's Word dwell richly in our lives.

People's Hearts Failing Is a Sign of the End of the Age

Looking again at our anchor verse in Luke 21:26, we see Jesus describing the end times, and He tells us that the last of the last days are going to be filled with so many traumatic events that "men's hearts [will be] failing them for fear, and for looking after those things which are coming on the earth...."

The truth is, if you look at the news, it can be quite overwhelming to see what is happening in the world. There are escalating wars in the Middle East and other parts of the world, there is rising inflation and debt, there are unprecedented attacks on our children through gender reassignment, and on and on the list goes. If you're not careful, issues like these and others can really cause you to lose your peace.

What we are seeing is what Jesus said would take place at the very end of the age: Men's hearts are beginning to fail. The word "fail" in Luke 21:26 means *to faint for fear*, and that is what's happening because of the things people are seeing.

Yet, despite all the negative circumstances we see, we don't have to lose heart or lose our peace. We can still have peace of mind even in troubled times.

The Peace of God Is To Rule Our Hearts

Rick and Denise are no strangers to troubling, traumatic events. Having lived on the other side of the world in the former Soviet Union for more than three decades, they have faced an array of difficulties, and their autobiography *Unlikely* tells their story.

Through all that they have endured, one of the verses that has really strengthened them is Colossians 3:15, which says:

And let the peace of God rule in your hearts....

According to this passage, the peace of God is supposed to rule in our hearts. But what does the word "peace" mean? Interestingly, it is the Greek word *eirene*, the same word we saw in John 14:27. In fact, this is the primary word for peace in the New Testament.

The meaning of this word *eirene* depicts *the cessation of war, an end of conflict*, and *a time of rebuilding and reconstruction after the war has ceased*. It is *a time when distractions are removed, a time of prosperity*, or *the rule of order in the place of chaos*.

The peace of God is *a calm, inner stability that results in the ability to conduct oneself peacefully even in the midst of circumstances that would normally be traumatic or upsetting.* The Greek word *eirene* is the equivalent for the Hebrew word *shalom*, which expresses the idea of *wholeness, completeness*, or *tranquility in the soul that is unaffected by outward circumstances or pressures*.

Friend, when you're ruled by peace, you're able to conduct yourself peacefully, even during circumstances that would normally be traumatic or upsetting. It means war has ended, conflict has ceased, and distractions have been removed. Rather than being focused on war and conflicts, you're focused on rebuilding and reconstructing and on the positive things of life.

Functioning in the peace of God means *shalom is ruling your soul*. You've been ushered into a time of peace and prosperity and out of the place of chaos.

When God's Peace Is Ruling, It Acts Like an *Umpire* in Your Life

Looking again at Colossians 3:15, we see that the apostle Paul instructed us, "...Let the peace of God *rule* in your hearts...." The word "rule" here is the unique Greek term *brabeuo*, which, in ancient times, described *the umpire or referee who moderated and judged the athletic competitions that were so popular in the ancient world.*

By using this word, Paul was telling us **the peace of God should work like an umpire or referee in our hearts, minds, and emotions**.

When negative emotions try to exert control over us or to throw us into an emotional frenzy, we can stop it from happening by making the choice to let God's supernatural peace rise up from deep inside us — like an umpire or referee — to moderate our emotions.

As we do, we will be kept under the control of divine peace as it rules in our hearts. When this divine umpire called "peace" steps into the game, it suddenly begins to call the shots and make all the decisions instead of fretfulness, anxiety, and worry.

When we insert the meaning of the Greek word *brabeuo* — translated here as "rule" — Colossians 3:15 could be translated:

- Let the peace of God *call the shots in your life....*

- Let the peace of God *be the umpire in your life and actions....*

- Let the peace of God *act as referee in your emotions and your decisions....*

What is calling the shots in your life right now? Is it your emotions or feelings? You need to be careful not to give in to your feelings because they will try to run your life. According to this verse, the peace of God is to call the shots and serve as an umpire or referee in your heart, your mind, and your decisions. His peace should determine what is allowed and what is not allowed in your life.

Rick Experienced God's Peace
Dominating His Soul at a Very Crucial Time

For Rick and Denise, peace ruling as an umpire is not just a theory, but a reality in their life. Years ago, they experienced an extremely bizarre situation in which someone in another country was trying to steal their ministry. In Rick's own words, here is their story:

> This person had legally registered everything in his name and had disguised his operations. It was a very clandestine effort to literally steal a part of our ministry out from under us.
>
> To handle the situation, members of my team and I flew to the part of the world where the plot was taking place. When we got there, what we experienced was beyond anything I'd ever faced in my life.
>
> As soon as we met and confronted the person who was trying to steal our operation, he began yelling, screaming, and threatening to call the police and have us arrested. The crazy thing is that I was in my own office!

Amazingly, as I stood there in the midst of all the chaos, the peace of God rose up on the inside of me and enabled me to remain calm.

My team, on the other hand, was not so peaceful. In fact, one of my associates was screaming so loudly, I thought he was going to get into a fist fight with the person who had wronged us. Meanwhile, another staff member was threatening to call our attorney and bring legal charges against the person.

Surprisingly, in the midst of all the yelling, the screaming, and the tsunami of emotions swirling in the room, I was peaceful. I vividly remember being in that situation and thinking, *Wow! Everyone has lost their cool, and you are like an island of peace in the middle of great conflict.*

The reason I remained calm, cool, and collected is because I was dominated by peace. I never got caught up in the war or the conflict, and none of the distractions affected me. I was able to think clearly and make the right decisions, even though I was in the midst of traumatic and upsetting events all around me.

As I assessed the situation and saw what was happening, I told my team to calm down, and they looked at me like I was a sign or a wonder because I was so visibly unaffected. But that's what happens when the peace of God acts as an umpire and calls the shots in your life. It determines what will and what will not rule you.

If I had let my emotions take advantage of me, that situation would have spiraled out of control and would have been very bad. But because I was ruled by the peace of God, I was able to remain peaceful, think clearly, and make the right decisions.

To God's credit, we came out of that situation fine and without a scratch. In fact, things ended up even better than they were previously. I am so grateful for the peace of God that was ruling and dominating my life.

The Peace of God Is Directly Connected With the Word of God

If you want the peace of God to rule your life as Colossians 3:15 says, you need to understand and put into practice what Paul said in the very next verse:

> **Let the word of Christ dwell in you richly....**
> — **Colossians 3:16**

The word "dwell" here is the Greek word *enoikeo*, a compound of *en* and *oikeo*. The word *en* means *in* or *inside*, and the word *oikeo* means *to live*. When we compound these two words to form *enoikeo*, it means *to live inside*, *to dwell inside*, or *to comfortably take up residency*.

By using the word *enoikeo*, this verse pictures the Word of God "taking up residency" and "living inside" us! It depicts someone so full of the Word of God that his entire being is affected. His heart is full of joy, his mind is flooded with wisdom and understanding, and his mouth is singing songs to the Lord. Having the peace of God rule as an umpire is directly connected with letting the Word feel at home in you and dwelling lavishly inside your heart.

The Word Is To Live in You 'Richly'

The way in which we welcome God's Word into our lives is also vital. Again, Paul instructed us, "Let the word of Christ dwell in you richly..."

(Colossians 3:16). In Greek, the word "richly" is the extraordinary word *plousios*, which describes *incredible abundance, extreme wealth, enormous affluence, great prosperity, immense riches, magnificent opulence,* or *extravagant lavishness.*

The word *plousios* pictures one who is *filthy, stinking rich,* and its use here communicates two things: First, it tells us how we are to receive God's Word — *richly.* We are to welcome the Word with great joy and extravagance. Second, the word *plousios* tells us what happens when we receive God's Word — it imparts riches into our lives on all levels.

Friend, when you receive the Word of God in the right way — giving it a warm reception and making it feel at home in your life — it will enrich you spiritually. In fact, **the Word of God can make you a spiritual "billionaire!"**

In Jesus, All of Us Hit the Jackpot!

Rick shared how when he was a boy, he used to spend a great deal of time at his Grandpa and Grandma Renner's house. His grandfather was a German immigrant, and when he arrived in the United States, he didn't have very much. That remained virtually unchanged during his life. Yet, although they didn't have much, they did the best they could with what they had.

In any case, when Rick went to his grandparents' house, one of their favorite TV shows to watch was *Let's Make a Deal.* Visit after visit, he would often find his place on the couch and watch the show along with them. On the show, contestants were randomly picked out of the audience and given the opportunity to "make a deal" with the show's host and win a prize.

Well, Grandpa and Grandma Renner would get so involved in the program that at some point — especially toward the end of the show — they would begin shouting at the contestants on the screen, telling them what to do to win the best prize.

The host would say, "Is it behind door number one, door number two, or door number three?"

"Door number two! Door number two!" Rick's grandpa would yell.

"No! It's behind door number three!" his grandma shouted. "Pick door number three!"

They got so excited about trying to guess where the hidden treasure was, and when the program was over, they would often speak between themselves and say, "Wow! Just imagine if we were on *Let's Make a Deal* and we hit the jackpot. What would our lives be like?"

Well, guess what? If you're a child of God, the deal is already made! When the Word of God dwells in you richly, you hit the jackpot! You don't have to guess what's behind door number one, door number two, or door number three because you have the greatest prize right inside you!

Friend, if you will open the door and roll out the red carpet for the Word of God, it will bring all kinds of spiritual riches inside you — including peace. *In Christ, you've already struck it rich!*

Taking into account the original Greek meaning, here is the *Renner Interpretive Version* (*RIV*) of the first part of Colossians 3:16:

> **Let the Word of God dwell in you richly! Throw open the doors, roll out the red carpet, and give it a grand reception! If you'll let the Word dwell in you in this way, it will produce an amazing amount of spiritual wealth in your life....**

Open Your Life to the Word of God

Part of the spiritual wealth that is imparted to you when you let the Word of God dwell in you richly is God's supernatural, conquering *peace* ruling your heart. Remember, Jesus said, "Peace I leave with you, my peace I give unto you..." (John 14:27). And that supernatural peace is supposed to dominate your life, acting as an umpire or referee that calls all the shots.

Friend, your life is not to be dominated by your emotions or the feelings of others. Likewise, you are not to be tossed back and forth by all the crazy events happening in the world around you. Instead, God wants you to be ruled by peace. Remember Paul's instruction:

> **And let the peace of God rule in your hearts....**
> **— Colossians 3:15**

Again, this verse could be translated:

- Let the peace of God *call the shots in your life....*

- Let the peace of God *be the umpire in your life and actions....*

- Let the peace of God *act as referee in your emotions and your decisions....*

If you're tired of worrying and being anxious, open your life to the Word of God and let the Word dwell in you richly! Begin each day by reading your Bible and giving the Scripture a grand entrance into your mind and heart. Roll out the red carpet, and as the Word of God takes up residency in you, it will begin to impart to you all kinds of spiritual riches — including a dominating, supernatural peace that will call all the shots in your life.

In our next lesson, we are going to learn what it means to cast your care upon the Lord.

STUDY QUESTIONS

**Study to shew thyself approved unto God, a workman that
needeth not to be ashamed, rightly dividing the word of truth.**
— 2 Timothy 2:15

1. According to Colossians 3:15 and 16, the supernatural peace of God is directly connected to the Word of God. In fact, to fully experience God's peace, the Word of God must "take up residency" and "live inside" you. According to these promises in Scripture, what are some things you can expect to happen in your life as you "let the Word of Christ dwell in you richly"?

    - 2 Timothy 3:16 and 17

    - Romans 1:16

    - Hebrews 4:12

    - James 1:21-25

    - Joshua 1:8

2. Knowing of the amazing benefits of letting God's Word take up residency inside you, what practical steps might you take to create more space in your daily routine to read and study the Bible?

    If you're new to reading the Bible and don't have a version you understand, consider getting a translation you can better comprehend, such as the *New Living Translation*, the *New International Version*, or the *Living Bible*. If you struggle to read consistently or don't really have a desire to be in the Word, pray and tell the Lord about it. Ask

Him to give you a desire, and then be disciplined to get into the Word and consistently feed your spirit and soul. The more you read it, the more your desire will grow. He will answer your request!

PRACTICAL APPLICATION

> **But be ye doers of the word, and not hearers only,**
> **deceiving your own selves.**
> **—James 1:22**

Take time to meditate on Colossians 3:15 in the *Amplified Bible, Classic Edition*, which helps capture the original meaning of the verse:

> **And let the peace (soul harmony which comes) from Christ rule (act as umpire continually) in your hearts [deciding and settling with finality all questions that arise in your minds, in that peaceful state] to which as [members of Christ's] one body you were also called [to live]. And be thankful (appreciative), [giving praise to God always].**

1. What is the Holy Spirit showing you about the role of peace as the "umpire" of your life?
2. Think about what an umpire in baseball does and how much weight his decisions carry. He determines what is *foul, safe,* or *out*. How does this comparison help you better understand what peace is meant to do in your mind, emotions, and decisions?
3. If your emotions are *running* your life, they are likely *ruining* your life. If that is the case, it's time to press on the brakes and say, "Stop! I'm not going to live like this anymore." Pray and invite the Holy Spirit who lives inside you to show you and help you make peace the umpire of your life — deciding and settling with finality all questions that arise in your mind.

TOPIC

Cast All Your Care Upon the Lord

SCRIPTURES

1. **Luke 21:26** — Men's hearts failing them for fear, and for looking after those things which are coming on the earth....

2. **1 Peter 5:7** — Casting all your care upon him; for he careth for you.

3. **Luke 19:35** — And they brought him to Jesus: and they cast their garments upon the colt, and they set Jesus thereon.

GREEK WORDS

1. "casting"— ἐπιρρίπτω (*epiripto*): a compound of ἐπι (*epi*) and ῥίπτω (*rhipto*); the word ἐπι (*epi*) means upon, as in on top of something, and the word ῥίπτω (*rhipto*) means to hurl, to throw, or to cast, and it often means to violently throw or to fling something with great force; as a compound, it means to hurl, to throw, or to cast; to throw or to fling something with great force; in secular literature it often pictured the flinging of a garment, bag, or excess weight off the shoulders of a traveler and onto the back of a beast, such as a donkey, camel, or horse

2. "care"— μέριμνα (*merimna*): anxiety; used to describe affliction, difficulty, hardship, misfortune, trouble, or a complicated circumstance that arises as a result of problems that develop in life; this could include problems that are financial, marital, job-related, family-related, business-oriented, or anything else that concerns us in the earthly realm

3. "careth"— μέλει (*melei*): to feel apprehensive; to be aware, to be concerned, to be interested, to notice, to be thoughtful, or to give meticulous attention

SYNOPSIS

Regardless of what you are going through or what is going on around you, it is God's will for His supernatural peace to rule and dominate your life, calling all the shots just as an umpire does in the game of baseball. His peace should decide with finality what is "in" and what is "out." If you have peace in your spirit about something, it is *in* — it is *safe*. If you don't have peace in your heart about something, it is *foul* and should be thrown *out* of your life.

Colossians 3:15 tells us to let *God's peace* rule. Although our emotions can be a blessing to us, they were never meant to run our lives. Instead, we are to take charge of our emotions and allow the peace of God to rule our mind, our emotions, and the decisions of our will.

The emphasis of this lesson:

Nothing in our life improves by worrying — it only makes everything worse. Jesus wants us to take all the things we are anxious, worried, and stressed about and heave them onto His shoulders. That is what it means to cast our cares on Him. He is extremely interested in and concerned about every facet of our lives.

Carefully Guard What You Are Watching and Listening To

We have noted in our previous lessons that in Luke 21:26, Jesus described one of the things that would be happening in the end times. He said, "Men's hearts [would be] failing them for fear, and for looking after those things which are coming on the earth...."

In today's information age, we have instant access to the news of what is happening all around the world. The problem is that most of what is reported is negative and deeply disturbing. There are problems everywhere, and if we continually watch and listen to everything that is going on, our hearts will begin to fail us for fear, just as Jesus prophesied.

Indeed, we are living in desperate, troubling times, which is why we really need to guard what we are watching and listening to. If you're watching so much news that it's stealing your peace, you need to turn it off.

A practical and biblical test to always measure your thoughts by is found in Philippians 4:8:

> **Finally, brethren, whatsoever things are true, whatsoever things are honest, whatsoever things are just, whatsoever things are pure, whatsoever things are lovely, whatsoever things are of**

good report; if there be any virtue, and if there be any praise, think on these things.

A Real-Life Lesson
In Learning To 'Cast Your Care' on Christ

In Lesson 1, Rick shared a testimony from his life of how God had charged him to build a church in the city of Riga, Latvia shortly after he and his family moved to that region. The Republic of Latvia had been part of the Soviet Union, and for that reason, no churches had been built for 55 years by the time Rick and his family arrived in 1991.

Although he immediately set out to obey God, he didn't know how they were going to carry out the task. Remarkably, the government gave Rick and his team permission to build the church, but there was one stipulation: The entire project would need to be completed and the building occupied within two years. If they failed to finish, they would lose the building, the land, and everything they had invested in it.

Rick and his team were already doing many things by faith. They were broadcasting the Word of God through a television program that aired in 11 time zones across the former Soviet Union. Paying for the airtime required a great deal of money, not to mention the manpower needed to produce the shows and answer the tons of letters that were pouring in from viewers.

Rick was also publishing and printing books and mailing them free of charge to people everywhere. The ministry was paying for the printing, the packaging, and the postage, which also required a mountain of money to make happen.

So while he was believing for enough money to continue sending out all the printed materials, he was also believing for the funds to build the new church building, which was a 4-million-dollar project that had to be completed in two years. If they failed to finish the job, they would lose everything.

The pressure was on. Day after day, week after week, Rick worried about where the millions of dollars in cash were going to come from to pay for the building and everything else they were doing. It wasn't long before he lost his peace, and a frenzy of fear set in. Each night as he lay in bed, he would roll back and forth, worrying about how they would get the money to complete the project.

Denise, Rick's wife, would often be awakened by his restlessness and would turn to him and ask him to be still. To that, he would reply, "Would you please worry with me! How can you just lay there and sleep peacefully when I'm so worried about where the money is going to come from to complete the church and carry on the ministry."

"Oh, would you just give it to the Lord," she would say, which really angered Rick.

"That's easy for you to say," Rick snapped back. "No one is calling *you* for all these payments. They're calling *me!*"

A wake-up call in the middle of the night. One night, when Rick was worrying and couldn't sleep, he got up and began pacing the floor, just as he had done so many times before. "Where are we going to find the money we need to do this?" he repeatedly muttered. In his heart, he knew God had asked him to build the church, but he just couldn't seem to break free from worrying.

The truth is, it is silly to worry about how you're going to pay for God's project. If God gives you something to do, He will finance it — period. In Rick's case, God was using the situation to require him to come up higher in his faith, which is what He will do at times in your life too.

It was now two o'clock in the morning, and as Rick continued his walk of worry around the apartment, he made his way down to his study, sat in his chair, and laid his head on the desk. He then began to pray, "Oh God, what are we going to do? We need more money, because payments are due this week. Lord, what are we going to do?"

As tears began to trickle down Rick's face, suddenly, he felt a little tap on his shoulder. When he turned to look, he saw that it was his son Joel, who was a young boy at that time. Wiping the tears from his face, Rick asked, "Joel, why are you up in the middle of the night?"

Joel looked at him and said, "Dad, why are you crying?"

"Your dad is just worried and a little fearful about our building project," Rick responded. "I just don't know where I'm going to get the money to do this." Again, the money was needed to pay for the church *God* had asked Rick to build. His efforts were out of obedience to what the Lord had told him to do.

In that moment, Joel looked up at Rick, put his hand on his hip, and said, "Dad, hasn't God proven Himself faithful to you yet? You just need to give it to the Lord." And with that, Joel turned around, went back to his bedroom, and went to sleep.

Rick sat at his desk stunned. His son had basically told him to *cast his care on the Lord*, reminding him that God had always been faithful in the past, and He would continue to be faithful in the present and the future. This was a major wake-up call for Rick, reminding him of the Lord's faithfulness and the need to put his trust in Him.

Cast Your Care Upon Jesus

Make no mistake: Worrying is not going to change or bring any improvements to your situation. The only thing it will do is magnify the problem in your mind and make you feel even more overwhelmed than ever. Instead of worrying, God wants us to cast our cares upon Jesus. He makes this clear in First Peter 5:7:

> **Casting all your care upon him; for he careth for you.**

In this passage, the word "casting" is a form of the Greek word *epiripto*, a compound of the word *epi* and *rhipto*. The word *epi* means *upon*, as in *on top of something*, and the word *rhipto* means *to hurl, to throw*, or *to cast*. Often, *rhipto* means *to violently throw or to fling something with great force*. When these two words are compounded to form *epiripto*, it means *to hurl, to throw*, or *to cast*; or *to throw or to fling something with great force*.

In secular literature, the word *epiripto* often pictured the flinging of a garment, bag, or excess weight off the shoulders of a traveler and onto the back of a beast, such as a donkey, camel, or horse. The only other verse in the entire New Testament where this word is used is in Luke 19:35, which talks about Jesus' triumphant entry into Jerusalem just before His crucifixion. Here the Bible says:

> **And they brought him to Jesus: and they cast their garments upon the colt, and they set Jesus thereon.**

This passage is noteworthy because the words "cast...upon" are translated from a form of the Greek word *epiripto*, the same word translated as "casting" in First Peter 5:7. This gives us an accurate, vivid depiction of what *epiripto* means. Here we see the disciples of Jesus literally casting or throwing their garments on the back of the beast. Each one took an item of clothing off themselves and hurled them onto the donkey to carry.

Friend, we are not designed to carry the burden of worry, fretting, and anxiety. It's simply too much for the human body and the central nervous system to tolerate. We may be able to manage it for a while, but eventually the physical body and mind will begin to break under this type of perpetual pressure.

In fact, the medical world has confirmed that the major source of sickness in the Western Hemisphere is stress and pressure. Man was simply not fashioned to carry pressures, stresses, anxieties, and worries. This is the reason the body breaks down when it undergoes these negative influences for too long. If you are struggling with sickness or depression, your condition could very possibly be related to stress and pressure.

Jesus Wants To Be Your 'Beast of Burden'

Rather than carry the weight of worry, anxiety, and pressure that is breaking us down and emotionally distressing us, we're supposed to cast it over onto the Lord. In fact, in First Peter 5:7, it is almost as if Jesus is calling out to us and saying: "Your shoulders are not big enough to carry the burdens you're trying to bear by yourself. This load will eventually break you — so please let ME be your beast of burden! Take that load and heave it with all your might. Fling it over onto MY back, and let ME carry it for you!"

Just as Luke 19:35 says the disciples cast their garments upon the back of the donkey, now you need to cast your burdens over onto the Lord and let Him carry them for you! It is as if Jesus is literally saying, "Let ME be your beast of burden! I'll carry it all for you."

This doesn't mean all your problems go away. It just means they are transferred off of you and onto the shoulders of Jesus. He is walking alongside you, offering to carry the load. If you heave your load onto Him, you will move out of a lack of peace and come out from under the weight and pressure of anxiety, worry, and trying to figure everything out on your own.

What 'Cares' Are You To Cast on Jesus?

If you are wondering what kind of things you are to throw on the shoulders of Jesus, First Peter 5:7 makes it clear. Again, this verse says, "Casting all your care upon him; for he careth for you."

The word "care" here is a form of the Greek word *merimna*, which is *anxiety*. It was used to describe *affliction, difficulty, hardship, misfortune, trouble, or a complicated circumstance that arises as a result of problems that develop in one's life.* This could include problems that are financial, marital, job-related, family-related, business-oriented, or anything else that concerns us in the earthly realm.

Basically, a "care" is *anything that causes stress.* This means anything that causes you worry or anxiety — regardless of why it happened — is what you need to throw over onto the shoulders of Jesus Christ! Nothing is too big or small to talk to the Lord about because, "…He careth for you" (1 Peter 5:7).

The word "careth" is the Greek word *melei*, which means *to feel apprehensive, to be aware, to be concerned, to be interested, to notice, to be thoughtful,* or *to give meticulous attention.* Peter uses this word to assure us that Jesus really does care about us and the things that are heavy on our hearts. In fact, He is hovering over us right now, giving meticulous attention to what is happening to us.

Friend, He is interested in every facet of your life. He's feeling apprehensive about the fact that you're trying to carry the load by yourself. He's thoughtful and concerned for you in your situation, and that's why He's pleading to you through this verse, "Let Me be your beast of burden! If you keep carrying this by yourself, it's going to break you, but I'm right at your side. My shoulders are well able to carry all of it. Heave it over onto Me. I will carry it for you, and you can be free of it all."

When we insert the original Greek meaning, the *Renner Interpretive Version* (*RIV*) of First Peter 5:7 says:

> **Take that heavy burden, difficulty, or challenge you are carrying — the ones that have arisen due to circumstances that have created hardship and struggles in your life — and fling those worries and anxieties over onto the back of the Lord and let Him**

carry them for you! The Lord is extremely interested in every facet of your life, and He is genuinely concerned about your welfare.

So don't ever let the devil tell you that your problems are too stupid, small, or insignificant to bring to Jesus. The Lord is interested in everything that concerns you!

Jesus Really Cares About You!

As difficult as that season was for Rick when he was building the church in Riga, Latvia, God used the situation to really make him aware of just how much the Lord cares for us. Reflecting on what the Holy Spirit showed him, Rick said:

> When I saw these Greek words in First Peter 5:7 and perceived how deeply Jesus cared about the burdens that were on my heart, I realized I was carrying a load I didn't have to bear by myself. Jesus was standing right at my side, longing to help me and inviting me to shift the weight from my shoulders onto His.
>
> By faith, I heaved those financial cares onto the back of Jesus — and when I did, I was set free from the stress, anxiety, and pressure that had been weighing me down at that time in my life.

You don't have to carry the whole weight of the world by yourself. Jesus loves you so much and is so deeply concerned about you and the difficulties you are facing that He is calling out to you right now and is saying: "Roll those burdens over onto Me and let Me carry them for you so you can be free!"

If you are lugging around worries, cares, and concerns about your family, your business, your church, or any other area of your life, why not stop right now and say, "Jesus, I'm yielding every one of these concerns to You today. I cast my burden on You, and I thank You for setting me free!"

In our next lesson, we will learn the importance of keeping the devil under your feet, which is where he belongs.

STUDY QUESTIONS

> **Study to shew thyself approved unto God, a workman that needeth not to be ashamed, rightly dividing the word of truth.**
> **— 2 Timothy 2:15**

1. Jesus had a great deal to say about worry, a habit most of us have struggled with on occasion. Take some time to carefully reflect on what He said in Matthew 6:25-34 and Luke 12:22-31 about *not* worrying, and jot down your greatest takeaways. What verse(s) speaks to you the loudest? Why?

2. Fear of running out and not having the money or resources we need can be overwhelming. Thankfully, God has answers to this peace-stealing line of thinking. Check out what He promises in these powerful passages:

   - Romans 8:31,32
   - 2 Corinthians 9:8
   - Philippians 4:19
   - Psalm 34:9,10; 84:11
   - Hebrews 13:5,6

PRACTICAL APPLICATION

> **But be ye doers of the word, and not hearers only, deceiving your own selves.**
> **— James 1:22**

1. More than likely, you have had overwhelming challenges in the past that you didn't see any way out of — but today you are no longer in them. If you were to pick the most stressful situation, which would it be? What were some of the biggest worries that were stealing your peace? How did God deliver you out of it, and what did He teach you? How does remembering His faithfulness give you hope and encouragement for what you're currently facing?

2. It is a medically proven fact that most sicknesses in the Western world are the result of stress and pressure that our soul and body were not meant to bear. Take a few moments to be still in God's presence and pray, "Lord, what pressures, stresses, anxieties, and worries am I trying to carry on my own? What cares and burdens do I need to take

off of myself and heave onto You?" Listen for what He shows you, and then cast them onto Jesus, who longs to be your beast of burden.

TOPIC
Keep the Devil Where He Belongs — Under Your Feet!

SCRIPTURES

1. **Ephesians 6:14,15** — Stand therefore, having your loins girt about with truth, and having on the breastplate of righteousness; and your feet shod with the preparation of the gospel of peace.
2. **Romans 16:20** — And the God of peace shall bruise Satan under your feet shortly....

GREEK WORDS

1. "shod" — ὑποδέω (*hupodeo*): a compound of the words ὑπο (*hupo*) and δέω(*deo*); the word ὑπο (*hupo*) means under, and the word δέω (*deo*) means to bind; as a compound, it conveys the idea of binding something very tightly on the bottom of one's feet; this is not the picture of a loosely fitting shoe, but of a shoe that has been tied onto the bottom of the foot extremely tightly

2. "bruise" — συντρίβω (*suntribo*): to crush; to smash; used to depict the smashing of bones or the crushing of grapes into wine

3. "shortly" — τάχος (*tachos*): when used in connection to the marching of Roman soldiers, it is used to depict the pounding steps of soldiers as they walked in formation

4. "preparation"— ἑτοιμασία (*etoimasia*): when used in connection with Roman soldiers, the word portrayed men of war who had their shoes tied on very tightly to ensure a firm footing; once they had the assurance that their shoes were going to stay in place, they were ready to march out onto the battlefield and confront the enemy

SYNOPSIS

Did you know that there are seven specific pieces of armor God has provided for you to defend yourself and defeat the enemy? Paul talks about them in his letter to the believers in Ephesus. What is interesting is that one of the weapons in our arsenal that he mentions is *peace*. When we understand the power of peace and tie it tightly to our lives, it enables us to deal the devil a crushing defeat and keep him under our feet where he belongs!

The emphasis of this lesson:

The peace of God is a powerful weapon we've been given in our fight against the enemy. Peace tied tightly to our lives as believers is like the killer shoes of a Roman soldier. It protects us from being bruised and slashed by the enemy's attacks and keeps us grounded in faith and sure-footed in our walk with God.

You Can Be at Peace Despite What Is Happening

No one is more accurate in predicting the future than Jesus Himself. In Luke 21:26, He gave us some details about what will be taking place at the end of the age, telling us, "Men's hearts [would be] failing them for fear, and for looking after those things which are coming on the earth...."

The word "failing" here means *to faint*, which tells us that in the end times, people are going to witness such bizarre things coming on the earth that the sight of it will cause their hearts to faint. Although every generation before us has witnessed their own share of strange developments, we are living at a time when multiple developments are being compounded one upon the other and happening all at once. As a result, men's hearts are failing them just as Jesus said in Luke 21:16.

Thankfully, the Lord has provided us with the antidote for these disturbing events, and it is His peace. He said, "Peace I leave with you, my peace I give unto you: not as the world giveth, give I unto you. Let not your heart be troubled, neither let it be afraid" (John 14:27).

We saw that the word "give" describes *a gift*, which means Jesus has gifted you with His peace, and it is so powerful that it will enable you to be like an island of peace even when you feel surrounded by a sea of trouble.

You don't have to be caught up in the fray of all the difficulty happening around you. Instead, you can remain in peace, which is God's will for your life.

Through Christ, You Have Peace *With* God

It is important to note that there are two kinds of peace talked about in Scripture. The first is *peace with God*, which is what we all receive the moment we repent of our sin and invite Jesus to be our Lord and Savior. The apostle Paul clearly describes peace with God in Romans 5:1 where he says:

> **Therefore being justified by faith, we have *peace with God* through our Lord Jesus Christ.**

The Bible tells us that before we were born again, we were enemies of God (*see* Romans 5:10). But through Jesus' death and resurrection, the enmity or hostility between us and the Father has been removed (*see* Ephesians 2:15,16). The score was settled, and the price for our sin was paid on the Cross.

Through the shed blood of Jesus, we now have *peace with God*, and our relationship with Him is fully restored. When we put our faith in Christ, we are instantly redeemed and become God's sons and daughters (*see* John 1:12,13). Praise His mighty Name!

Through Christ, You Are Armed With the Peace *of* God

The second kind of peace described in Scripture is the *peace of God*, which is His powerful, keeping peace. Many people are at peace *with* God, but they do not have the peace *of* God working in their lives. They're in distress, filled with anxiety, and overwhelmed by worry, which is the total opposite of what God wants us — His children — to experience.

God's will is for you to walk and live in His keeping peace, regardless of what is going on around you. That is what Jesus offers us in John 14:27. His peace is so powerful it is actually one of the weapons we have been given to win in our warfare against the enemy. The apostle Paul talked about this in Ephesians 6:14 and 15 where he instructed us:

Stand therefore, having your loins girt about with truth, and having on the breastplate of righteousness; and your feet shod with the preparation of the gospel of peace.

Here Paul described a Roman soldier who is standing tall with his head held high, shoulders thrown back, and his chest heaved forward. This soldier knows who he is, and he is proud of it. Similarly, God wants you to really know who you are in Christ. You are a soldier in His army with absolutely no need to be ashamed or afraid of anything.

Notice that *truth* is the first weapon mentioned, and like the Roman soldier's belt, truth is given to us to hold our lives securely in place. Next, we see the breastplate of righteousness, which figuratively depicts the *righteousness* of Jesus guarding the core of our being — which is everything vital to our existence, including our heart, the very core of who we are. The third piece of armor we have been given is the shoes of peace, which is what we will focus on for the remainder of this lesson.

The Peace of God Is Like 'Killer Shoes'

Writing under the inspiration of the Holy Spirit, the apostle Paul said that your feet are to be "…shod with the preparation of the gospel of peace" (Ephesians 6:15). If you had seen the shoes of a Roman soldier, nothing about them looked peaceful. In fact, you would have wanted to make sure you didn't fall down in front of him or get in his way where he might accidentally step on you.

Those soldier's shoes weren't normal — they were killer shoes! They were made of two primary parts: one part was called the *greave* and the other was the *shoe* itself.

The greaves provided protection to the soldier's legs.

They were the portions of the shoes that covered a soldier's legs from his knees to his feet and were made of metal. They were specially shaped to wrap tightly around the soldier's calves and shins and were essential for the safekeeping of his legs. There are two reasons for these greaves on a soldier's legs.

First, the metal that covered his legs from his knees to the top of his feet was designed to protect his calves when he was required to march through rocky and thorny terrain. If he'd had no protection on his legs, he would have been gashed, cut, and bruised by the environment. Thus, the greaves gave the soldier protection so he could keep walking regardless of the obstacles he encountered.

Second, the greaves gave him defensive protection in those moments when an adversary kicked him in the shins, trying to break his legs. If a soldier could be knocked to the ground, his opponent could more easily take off his head. Thus, the greaves covered and protected the soldier's calves and shins so his legs could not be broken, rendering useless the enemy's attacks.

Our spiritual "greaves" protect us from being bruised and slashed by the enemy.

As a believer, you have been provided with spiritual "greaves," and they are designed to protect you through rough and tough situations, which you will face at various times in your life. Some of the difficulties you face and must walk through are very *thorny*. These include the sharp, piercing problems found in your relationships, your job, and even the Church.

If you make it past the thorny situations in life, you will sometimes run into very rocky times. Financial struggles, health issues, and relational challenges can all be very hard and have the potential to leave you emotionally and mentally bruised. The enemy sends one bad event after another, trying to break your legs and bring you down so he can defeat you.

Without the peace of God, you will be injured. But just as the greaves of a Roman soldier protected him from the environment and from the blows of his enemy, the peace of God — when it is operating in your life — protects and defends you from the hassles and assaults of the devil.

The enemy may try to disrupt you, distract you, and steal your attention by causing negative events to whirl all around you, but his attempts will fail because the peace of God, like a protective greave, will prevent you from being hurt and enable you to keep marching forward!

Amazingly, God's supernatural peace is so potent that it can sometimes shield you in such a way that you don't even know you're under attack. His peace acts like a divine bubble, which is just the kind of protection we need in these last days.

The soldier's shoe itself was worn around the foot. This second part was made of heavy pieces of leather that were tied together with leather straps. The bottom of the shoes was affixed with sharp, dangerous, protruding spikes called hobnails that gripped the ground. Extending beyond the front of each shoe were two additional sharply pointed spikes. All these spikes had several purposes.

First, the spikes on the bottom of the soldier's shoes were intended to hold him "in place" when in battle. His opponent might try to push him around, but the spikes on the bottom of his shoes helped keep him securely grounded, making the soldier virtually immovable.

Additionally, those spikes on the bottom and front of the shoes served as weapons of brutality and murder. One good kick with those shoes, and that opponent would be dead. Likewise, just a few seconds of stomping on a fallen adversary would have eradicated that foe forever!

Roman soldiers tied their shoes tightly to their feet.

Again, Ephesians 6:15, says, "And your feet shod with the preparation of the gospel of peace." This odd word "shod" is from a form of the Greek word *hupodeo*, a compound of the words *hupo* and *deo*. The word *hupo* means *under*, and the word *deo* means *to bind*. As a compound, *hupodeo* conveys the idea of *binding something very tightly on the bottom of one's feet*.

Hence, this is not the picture of a loosely fitting shoe, but a shoe that has been tied onto the bottom of the foot extremely tightly. These shoes gave the Roman soldier sure footing. He was never afraid of losing his shoes.

In the same way, we need to be sure that the peace of God is a real fixture in our life. It can't be an accessory we haphazardly or loosely attach. Peace must be an anchor to which we are tightly tied. Only then will it not be lost and give us sure footing so that we can move with ease and speed into the things God has called us to do.

Shoes of peace keep us anchored in Christ.

Just as those spikes held a Roman soldier securely in place when his enemy tried to push him around, the peace of God will hold you in place whenever the devil tries pushing you around. Although he will try everything in his power to move you out of your position, the shoes of peace will keep you firmly planted and immovable!

Have you ever seen a palm tree in a hurricane? It bends and bends, first this way then that way, but it never surrenders its position because its roots hold it in place. When the hurricane finally ends, the palm tree just pops right back into place and never loses its position.

Likewise, when you have the peace of God operating in your life, it enables you to stay put. Of course, the devil doesn't want you to stay put. He wants you to surrender, give up, and move away from the promises of God. He wants you to move out of peace, but real peace holds you in place.

Paul thus told us that we must firmly tie God's peace onto our lives. If we only give peace a loosely fitting position in our lives, it won't be long before the affairs of life knock our peace out of place. That means we must bind peace onto our minds and emotions in the same way Roman soldiers made sure to bind their shoes very tightly onto their feet.

Walking in Peace Strikes a Crushing Blow to the Enemy

Just as the soldier used the spikes on the bottom of his shoes to kick and to kill his opponent, you are to march forward in peace and stomp all over the enemy if he is foolish enough to get in your way! By the time you're finished using your shoes of peace, you won't have much of a devil problem to deal with anymore!

The apostle Paul referred to this in Romans 16:20 where he declared, "And the God of peace shall bruise Satan under your feet shortly...." In this passage, the word "bruise" is from a form of the Greek word *suntribo*, which means *to crush* or *to smash*. Interestingly, it was used to depict the smashing of bones or the crushing of grapes into wine. Thus, it describes the absolute obliteration of something.

The use of this word *suntribo* means we could translate Romans 16:20 this way: "And the God of peace shall *smash*, shall *crush*, and shall *pulverize and obliterate* Satan under your feet shortly...."

This brings us to the word "shortly," which is translated from a form of the Greek word *tachos*. When used in connection to the marching of a Roman solider, it depicted *the pounding steps of soldiers as they walked in parade formation.*

When Roman soldiers marched, they pounded their feet on the pavement and the rocks to signal that they were coming through. Remember, they had spikes on the bottom of their shoes, so if someone fell in front of them, they didn't stop and politely ask the person to move. These were Roman soldiers, and they didn't stop for anyone. They just kept pounding and stomping as they marched all over that person.

Can you imagine what someone who fell in the middle of the road might look like after hundreds of Roman soldiers pounded their way through the streets? By the time the soldiers had passed through, that person would likely be crushed beyond recognition. That is the prophetic picture God is painting to tell us what happens to the enemy when we walk in peace.

Take Your Place As God's 'Man of War'

The devil is a demanding dictator, always telling us things like, "You'd better stop! You'd better back up! Don't come any closer!" But when you're keeping the peace of God, you can keep marching, and if the devil is dumb enough to get in your way, just knock him flat to the ground. Then stomp and bruise him under your feet, marching all the way through to victory.

There is one more thing you need to see in Ephesians 6:15. When it says, "And your feet shod with the preparation of the gospel of peace," the Greek word for "preparation" is *etoimasia*, and it was used in connection with Roman soldiers. This word portrayed *men of war who had their shoes tied on very tightly to ensure a firm footing*. Once they had the assurance that their shoes were going to stay in place, they were ready to march out onto the battlefield and confront the enemy.

As a believer, when peace is securely fastened in your life, it gives you the assurance you need to step out in faith and make the moves God is leading you to make. Before you take those steps, you need to be sure His peace is operating in your life.

Shoes of peace are a mighty and powerful piece of your God-given spiritual weaponry. Without it, the devil can effectively kick, punch, pull, and distract you. But with God's conquering peace firmly tied to your mind and emotions, you will be empowered to keep marching ahead, and you will be fortified against the devil's attempts to take you down!

In our final lesson, we will focus on five important steps to move you from turmoil to peace.

STUDY QUESTIONS

Study to shew thyself approved unto God, a workman that needeth not to be ashamed, rightly dividing the word of truth.
— 2 Timothy 2:15

1. God wants you to know who you are in Christ Jesus and declare it aloud over your life. This will release a greater level of peace within you. Are there any specific characteristics God has shown you about your identity in Christ? If so, what are they? What scriptures relate to these qualities?

2. To help you better understand who you are in Jesus, here are a few passages that identify some key characteristics of what you've been given through your faith in Him:
   - 2 Corinthians 5:17
   - 2 Corinthians 5:21
   - Romans 8:1,2
   - 1 Corinthians 6:11
   - Ephesians 2:5,6
   - Ephesians 2:10
   - Colossians 2:10

PRACTICAL APPLICATION

But be ye doers of the word, and not hearers only, deceiving your own selves.
— James 1:22

1. As you read through the detailed comparison between the Roman soldier's shoes, or greaves, and the peace of God, what stood out and impacted you most? How does this comparison help you understand and better appreciate the gift of God's peace?

2. We know from Scripture that the peace of God comes from Him — it is Jesus' gift to us and the fruit of His Spirit in our life (*see* John 14:27; Psalm 29:11; Galatians 5:22,23). For peace to keep you firmly grounded in Christ and function as a weapon against the enemy, you must pursue peace (*see* Psalm 34:14; Hebrews 12:14) and tie it tightly to your life.

According to Isaiah 26:3 and 4, what are two things that God promises will help you experience greater peace?

3. How is this lesson motivating you to expand your understanding of God's peace and pray more earnestly for His peace to be present in your life?

TOPIC

Five Important Steps To Move You From Turmoil to Peace

SCRIPTURES

1. **Luke 21:26** — Men's hearts failing them for fear, and for looking after those things which are coming on the earth....

2. **Philippians 4:6** — Be careful for nothing; but in every thing by prayer and supplication with thanksgiving let your requests be made known unto God.

3. **John 1:1** — In the beginning was the Word, and the Word was with God....

4. **James 5:16** — ...The effectual fervent prayer of a righteous man availeth much.

5. **Philippians 4:7** — And the peace of God, which passeth all understanding, shall keep your hearts and minds through Christ Jesus.

GREEK WORDS

1. "prayer" — προσευχή (*proseuche*): close, up-front, intimate contact; coming close to express a wish, desire, prayer, or vow; it was originally used to depict a person who vowed to give something of great value to God in exchange for a favorable answer to prayer; it portrays an individual who desires to see his prayer answered so desperately that he is willing to surrender everything he owns in exchange for answered prayer; hence, contained in this word is the concept of surrender

2. "supplication" — δέησις (*deisis*): depicts a person who has some type of lack in his life and therefore pleads strongly for his lack to be met; translated several ways in the King James Version, including to beseech, to beg, or to earnestly appeal; pictures a person in such great need that he feels compelled to push his pride out of the way so he can boldly, earnestly, strongly, and passionately cry out for someone to help or assist him

3. "thanksgiving" — εὐχαριστία (*eucharistia*): a compound of the words εὐ (*eu*) and χαρίζομαι (*charidzomai*); the word εὐ (*eu*) means good or well and denotes a general good disposition or an overwhelmingly good feeling about something; the word χαρίζομαι (*charidzomai*) is the Greek word for grace or gratefulness; when compounded, the word εὐχαριστία (*eucharistia*) describes an outpouring of grace and of wonderful feelings that freely flow from the heart in response to someone or something

4. "requests" — αἰτέω (*aiteo*): portrays a person who insists or demands that a specific need be met after approaching and speaking to his superior with respect and honor; additionally expresses the idea that one possesses a full expectation to receive what was firmly requested; this word describes someone who prays authoritatively, in a sense demanding something from God; he knows what he needs and is so filled with faith that he isn't afraid to boldly come into God's presence to ask and expect to receive what he has requested

5. "known" — γνωρίζω (*gnoridzo*): to broadcast, to declare, to make a thing known, or to make something very evident

6. "peace" — εἰρήνη (*eirene*): depicts the cessation of war, an end of conflict, a time of rebuilding and reconstruction after war has ceased, a time when distractions are removed, a time of prosperity, or the rule of order in the place of chaos; a calm, inner stability that results in the ability to conduct oneself peacefully even in the midst of circumstances that would normally be traumatic or upsetting; the Greek equivalent for the Hebrew word shalom, which expresses the idea of wholeness, completeness, or tranquility in the soul that is unaffected by outward circumstances or pressures

7. "passeth" — ὑπερέχω (*huperecho*): to hold above and beyond all else; excelling; surpassing

8. "understanding" — νοῦς (*nous*): the mind

9. "keep" — **φρουρέω** (*phroureo*): pictures guards who either blocked or gave permission for entrance to a city

SYNOPSIS

Have you ever played the game of tag? Variations of it have been around since about the Fourth Century B.C. One person is "it," and the rest of the participants do their best to run, hide, and not be touched by the one who is "it." Eventually everyone playing gets tagged, and the last one tagged during the game is "it" for the next round.

In many ways, the people of the world throughout all generations have been involved in a game of tag, and from all the signs we see around us currently, it seems that God has tapped our generation and said, "*Tag, you're it!* You are the generation to live at the end of the age!" This means that we are going to see things coming on the earth — very disturbing things — that no previous generation has ever seen before.

Jesus talked about this in Luke 21:26, prophesying, "Men's hearts [would be] failing them for fear, and for looking after those things which are coming on the earth…." But as a child of God, you don't have to be troubled or afraid. Why? Because Jesus said, "Peace I leave with you, my peace I give unto you…" (John 14:27).

Peace has been gifted to you by Jesus, and it is God's will that you be in peace regardless of the troubling times in which you are living. In this final lesson, we will focus on five important steps to move you from turmoil into peace.

The emphasis of this lesson:

At the first sign of anxiety, worry, or fear, run to God in prayer and give it to Him in exchange for His help. Ask boldly, passionately, and respectfully, making sure your thankfulness equals your request. When your request is based on God's Word, you can broadcast it boldly, insisting He meet your need. His peace will serve as a guardian of your heart and mind, keeping out everything that tries to steal your peace.

God's Proven Plan for Peace
Is Found in Philippians 4:6

One of the greatest verses to help us stay in peace and live free from worry and fear is Philippians 4:6. Here, under the anointing of the Holy Spirit, the apostle Paul laid out God's proven plan for peace, telling us boldly:

> **Be careful for nothing; but in every thing by prayer and supplication with thanksgiving let your requests be made known unto God.**

In the original Greek, the phrase "be careful for nothing" literally means *do not worry about anything at all*. Paul tells us what we should do instead of worrying: "…In every thing by prayer and supplication with thanksgiving let your requests be made known unto God" (Philippians 4:6). The words "in every thing" are a translation from the Greek word that signifies *every little detail of your life*.

As we learned in our previous lesson, First Peter 5:7 tells us that God is mindful and deeply concerned with every little detail of your life. Although counselors can certainly help us work through difficult issues, the first person we should go to with our problems is the Lord because only He has the ability to effectively hear us and help us.

Philippians 4:6 makes it clear that we are to go to the Lord as often as needed and discuss every little detail and facet of our life. The verse then gives us five steps, which are marked by five key words, to walk free from turmoil and into peace. Those five words are:

1) prayer
2) supplication
3) thanksgiving
4) requests
5) known

STEP 1:
In every thing by *prayer…*

After we are instructed to "be careful for nothing," we are given the first step to take whenever something comes against our mind to steal our peace, and that is to *pray*. The word "prayer" is the Greek word *proseuche*, a compound of the words *pros* and *euche*. The word *pros* describes *up-close, face-to-face*, or *intimate contact*. It portrays the intimate relationship that exists between the members of the Godhead — God the Father, Jesus the Son, and the Holy Spirit.

John 1:1 says, "In the beginning was the Word, and the Word was *with* God…." The word "with" is taken from the word *pros*. By using this word to describe the relationship between the Father and the Son, the Holy Spirit is telling us that theirs is an intimate relationship. One expositor has translated this verse, "In the beginning was the Word, and the Word was *face to face* with God…."

The second part of the word *proseuche* is taken from the old Greek word *euchomai*, which describes *a wish, desire, prayer, or vow*. It was originally used to depict a person who made some kind of vow to God because of a need or desire in his or her life. It portrays an individual who desires to see his prayer answered so desperately that he's willing to surrender something of great value in exchange for a favorable answer to prayer. Hence, inherent in this word is the concept of *surrender*.

When the words *pros* and *euche* are compounded to form *proseuche*, it describes coming to a place of *close, up-front, face-to-face contact with God and expressing a wish, desire, prayer, or vow*. Of all the words used in the New Testament for prayer, this word *proseuche* is used most often. It carries the idea of an altar or a place of exchange where we come intimately close to God and bring Him our worries, concerns, and fears and then ask Him for His peace in exchange.

Here we see that when you're in a place of turmoil, you need to draw near to the altar of God (*pros*), and once you come intimately close to Him, you make a vow in exchange for His answer to your prayer (*euche*). You need to be willing to say, "God, I'm going to give you my turmoil, and in exchange, I'm asking You to give me Your peace." Remember, for you to obtain the peace that you need, you may need to surrender a few things, all of that is contained in this word *prayer*.

STEP 2:
In every thing by prayer and *supplication*…

The second step is "supplication," which is translated from a form of the Greek word *deisis*. This is the second most often used word in the New Testament for prayer. This word depicts *a person who has some type of lack in his life and therefore pleads strongly for his lack to be met.* It is translated several ways in the *King James Version*, including *to beseech, to beg,* or *to earnestly appeal.* It pictures a person in such great need that he feels compelled to push his pride out of the way so he can boldly, earnestly, strongly, and passionately cry out for someone to help or assist him.

One of the most powerful examples of the word *deisis* is found in James 5:16, where it says, "...The effectual *fervent prayer* of a righteous man availeth much." Here, the word *deisis* is translated "fervent prayer." This is passionate, earnest, heartfelt, sincere prayer. It is coming to God on the most serious terms to strongly beseech Him to move and to meet a specific need you're facing.

By using this word *deisis*, we find that when we come to God, we're to push our pride out of the way, be strong in making our appeal, and say, "God, my situation is very, very serious, and I ask you to get involved and help me."

This word "supplication" — the Greek word *deisis* — means you are supposed to boldly bring every single detail of your life, including every problem, to God and talk to Him about what is going on, regardless of what it is. If it is bothering you, you're to bring it to the Lord and passionately plead for Him to move.

STEP 3:
With *thanksgiving...*

The third step to move you from turmoil to peace is extremely important, but many people miss it. Philippians 4:6 says that when you come to God in prayer and earnestly make your appeal, it should be with "thanksgiving." And the word "thanksgiving" is from a form of the amazing Greek word *eucharistia,* a compound of the words *eu* and *charidzomai.*

The word *eu* means *good* or *well* and *denotes a general good disposition or an overwhelmingly good feeling about something.* The word *charidzomai* is the Greek word for *grace* or *gratefulness.* When compounded, the word *eucharistia* describes *an outpouring of grace and of wonderful feelings that freely flow from the heart in response to someone or something.*

When you come to the altar to *pray* and surrender everything to God (step 1) and you're making *supplication,* earnestly and boldly crying out for help and telling God what you need (step 2), *your bold asking needs to be matched with extravagant thankfulness.* Although the request has only just been made and the manifestation isn't evident yet, it is appropriate to thank God for doing what you have requested.

Thanksgiving is the voice of faith.

Think about when your children or grandchildren come to you and ask for something. How does it make you feel inside when they thank you in advance for doing it? It touches your heart so deeply you want to move heaven and earth to give them what they need.

In contrast, one of the most difficult things to deal with is ungratefulness. If you've ever generously given to someone who never took the time to thank you for the sacrifice you made for him or her, then you know ingratitude is not enjoyable. No one is drawn to an ingrate or a person who has a sense of entitlement. That attitude is a major turnoff that closes the heart and repels us from people.

That is why this third step of thankfulness is so vital. When you come to God with a grateful heart for all He has already done, and thankfulness is pouring from your lips, that is the voice of faith. So don't just ask and ask and ask. Follow up your asking with *earnest thanksgiving!* Thank God in advance for hearing you and moving on your behalf to answer your prayer.

When you move into thankfulness, it moves you out of fear, anxiety, worry, and fret and into peace. Thankfulness changes the atmosphere. Now you're really on the way from turmoil to peace!

Before we go further, here's a quick recap of the first three steps:

Step 1: *Prayer.* Come to the altar of God and make an exchange. Give Him your turmoil in exchange for His peace.

Step 2: *Supplication.* Lay down your pride and just tell God exactly what you need earnestly, boldly, and unabashedly.

Step 3: *Thanksgiving.* Lift your voice and begin to thank God in advance for His help. Your level of thankfulness needs to match the level of your asking. Thankfulness is the voice of faith, and when you move into thankfulness, you're changing the atmosphere and moving out of turmoil and into peace.

STEP 4:
Let your *requests...*

The fourth step out of turmoil and into peace is found in the word "requests," which is translated from a form of the Greek word *aiteo*. This word portrays a person who insists or demands that a specific need be met after approaching and speaking to his superior with respect and honor.

To be clear, there is no disrespectfulness in these requests — only honor and respect. The insistence and demand for the need to be met is confidently anchored in the knowledge of what God has promised in His Word. As long as your prayer is based on Scripture, you can have the assurance that God hears you and will answer your request (*see* 1 John 5:14,15).

Additionally, this word *aiteo* expresses the idea that one possesses a full expectation to receive what was firmly requested. Moreover, it describes someone who prays adamantly and authoritatively, in a sense demanding something from God — especially tangible needs, such as food, shelter, money, and so on. This person knows what he needs and is so filled with faith that he isn't afraid to boldly come into God's presence to ask and expect to receive what he has requested.

That is the way God wants you to approach Him in prayer — with *respect, honor, faith,* and *confident expectation* that you will receive what you are asking for because He has already promised it in His Word.

STEP 5:
Let your requests be made *known* unto God

The fifth and final step to move you out of fear and doubt and into faith and peace is to "...let your requests be made known unto God" (Philippians 4:6). The word "known" here is a form of the Greek word *gnoridzo*, which means *to broadcast, to declare, to make a thing known,* or *to make something very evident.*

This plainly means that your asking can be extremely bold! You are to declare to God what you need and broadcast it so loudly that all of Heaven hears you when you pray.

When we insert the Greek meaning of these five key words into Philippians 4:6, the *Renner Interpretive Version* (*RIV*) says:

Don't worry about anything — and that means nothing at all! Instead, come before God and give Him the things that concern you so He can, in exchange, give you what you need or desire. Be bold to strongly, passionately, and fervently make your request known to God, making certain that an equal measure of thanksgiving goes along with your strong asking. You have every right to ask boldly, so go ahead and insist that God meet your need. When you pray, be so bold that there is no doubt your prayer was heard. Broadcast it! Declare it! Pray boldly until you have the assurance that God has heard your request!

You Will Have Supernatural PEACE When You Walk Out These Five Steps

Every time you obediently walk out the five steps of Philippians 4:6 — *prayer, supplication, thanksgiving,* and making your *requests known* — you will experience the extraordinary promise of Philippians 4:7:

And the peace of God, which passeth all understanding, shall keep your hearts and minds through Christ Jesus.

When you choose God's way to deal with doubt, fear, anxiety, and worry, it results in supernatural **peace**. The word "peace" in this verse is the Greek word *eirene,* the same word for "peace" we saw in John 14:27, Colossians 3:15, Romans 16:20, and Ephesians 6:15.

This word *eirene* — peace — depicts *the cessation of war, an end of conflict,* and *a time of rebuilding and reconstruction after war has ceased.* So rather than being focused on the turmoil and the problems surrounding you, allow God's peace to help you shift your focus into a positive direction of rebuilding and reconstruction.

This word "peace" describes *a time when distractions are removed, a time of prosperity,* or *the rule of order in the place of chaos.* It is *a calm, inner stability that results in the ability to conduct oneself peacefully even in the midst of circumstances that would normally be traumatic or upsetting.*

Furthermore, the Greek word *eirene* is the equivalent for the Hebrew word *shalom,* which expresses the idea of *wholeness, completeness,* or *tranquility in the soul that is unaffected by outward circumstances or pressures.* When you follow all five steps in Philippians 4:6, you will experience the wonderful peace of God that will fill your soul with *shalom*!

In fact, Philippians 4:7 says God's peace "passeth all understanding," and the word "passeth" is a form of the Greek word *huperecho*, which means *to hold above and beyond all else — something that is excelling and surpassing.*

The Bible says God's indescribable peace excels, surpasses, and goes beyond our "understanding." This word is translated from a form of the Greek word *nous*, which is the term for *the mind.* That's where all those troubling emotions enter and try to exalt themselves above the truth of God's Word (*see* 2 Corinthians 10:5). But when you walk out the five steps of Philippians 4:6, God's peace prevents those fears, doubts, and worries from nesting in your mind.

A Quick Recap of the Five Steps of Philippians 4:6:

Step 1: *Prayer* (*proseuche*). Come to the altar of God and make an exchange. Give Him your turmoil in exchange for His peace.

Step 2: *Supplication* (*deisis*). Lay down your pride and honestly tell God what you're dealing with and what you need. This pleading or appeal is earnest, bold, and without shame.

Step 3: *Thanksgiving* (*eucharistia*). Begin to thank God in advance for moving on your behalf. Your level of thankfulness needs to match the level of your asking. Thankfulness is the voice of faith, and when you move into thankfulness, you're changing the atmosphere and moving out of turmoil and into peace.

Step 4: *Requests* (*aiteo*). Your "ask" is an insistence and demand — with honor and respect — for what you specifically need. Your request is a confident expectation that you will receive what God has promised in His Word.

Step 5: *Known* (*gnoridzo*). Your requests to God are to be broadcasted, declared, made known, or made very evident until you have the assurance that God has heard your requests!

Let the Peace of God Be the Guardian of Your Heart and Mind

The proactive work of God's supernatural peace in your life "...shall keep your hearts and minds through Christ Jesus" (Philippians 4:7). The word "keep" here is a form of the Greek word *phroureo*, which is the ancient term used to describe soldiers who stood on guard at the entrance to the city.

These soldiers were empowered and given the authority to decide who could come in and who was denied entrance. If these guards decided someone could enter, they would move out of the way and allow the person in. However, if they identified someone as bad or evil, they would block the entrance so the perpetrator could not get in.

By using this word *phroureo* — translated as "keep" — we see that the peace of God will stand on guard at the gateway to your heart and mind. If something bad or evil tries to enter, God's peace will say, "No! You can't enter! You're trying to steal my peace, so you can't come in." On the other hand, if something good comes to the door of your mind and heart, the peace of God will move out of the way and allow it to come into your life.

Friend, if you will follow the five steps in Philippians 4:6, you will move from fear to faith, from turmoil to peace, and from defeat to victory! This is the practical, biblical pathway into the wonderful, supernatural peace of God that passes understanding. His peace will keep your heart and mind, serving as a guard to protect the entrance of the very core of your life.

STUDY QUESTIONS

Study to shew thyself approved unto God, a workman that needeth not to be ashamed, rightly dividing the word of truth.
— 2 Timothy 2:15

1. Bringing your *requests* to God means approaching Him with honor and respect, insisting that He meet your needs based on what He's promised in His Word. Isaiah 62:6 (*AMPC*) confirms this, saying:
   ...You who [are His servants and by your prayers] put the Lord in remembrance [of His promises], keep not silence.

Considering what you need from God, what promises from Scripture can you begin to boldly pray and confidently know He will answer? If needed, look up key words in a concordance or online Bible search engine to discover what God has promised you concerning your needs.

2. *Thanksgiving is the voice of faith!* To awaken a thankful attitude of gratitude, do what the psalmist says in **Psalm 77:11** and **12** (*NIV*): **I will remember the deeds of the Lord; yes, I will remember your miracles of long ago. I will consider all your works and meditate on all your mighty deeds.**

Take time to *purposely remember* the amazing things God has done in your life and family — the ways He's provided, protected, forgiven, been patient, and extended mercy and grace when you didn't deserve it. As the Holy Spirit brings those memories to mind, open your mouth and give God the thanks, the praise, and the glory He so rightfully deserves!

PRACTICAL APPLICATION
But be ye doers of the word, and not hearers only, deceiving your own selves.
— James 1:22

1. Have you ever wondered what you should pray about? God wants you to come and talk to Him about everything and anything that is bothering you, regardless of what it is. Whatever you're worrying about should be what you're praying about. Knowing this truth, what things have you kept from God because you thought they were too small or didn't want to bother Him? Take time now to voice these concerns, walking through the five steps of Philippians 4:6.

2. According to Philippians 4:6, the five key words that tell us exactly what we must do when worry and fear are trying to attack our hearts and minds are (1) *prayer*; (2) *supplication*; (3) *thanksgiving*; (4) *requests*; and (5) *known*. In your own words, describe each of these steps in God's proven plan for peace and tell which one touches your heart the most.

   • Pray

   • Bring supplication

- With thanksgiving
- Present requests
- Make known

3. As you complete this study, name at least one of your greatest take-aways that you want the Holy Spirit to permanently seal in your heart and mind.

Notes

Notes

A Prayer To Receive Salvation

If you've never received Jesus as your Savior and Lord, now is the time for you to experience the new life Jesus wants to give you! To receive God's gift of salvation that can be obtained through Jesus alone, pray this prayer from your heart:

> *Jesus, I repent of my sin and receive You as my Savior and Lord. Wash away my sin with Your precious blood and make me completely new. I thank You that my sin is removed, and Satan no longer has any right to lay claim on me. Through Your empowering grace, I faithfully promise that I will serve You as my Lord for the rest of my life.*

If you just prayed this prayer of salvation, you are born again! You are a brand-new creation in Christ! Would you please let us know of your decision by going to **renner.org/salvation**? We would love to connect with you and pray for you as you begin your new life in Christ.

Scriptures for further study: John 3:16; John 14:6; Acts 4:12; Ephesians 1:7; Hebrews 10:19,20; 1 Peter 1:18,19; Romans 10:9,10; Colossians 1:13; 2 Corinthians 5:17; Romans 6:4; 1 Peter 1:3

CLAIM YOUR FREE RESOURCE!

As a way of introducing you further to the teaching ministry of Rick Renner, we would like to send you FREE of charge his teaching, "How To Receive a Miraculous Touch From God" on CD or as an MP3 download.

In His earthly ministry, Jesus commonly healed *all* who were sick of *all* their diseases. In this profound message, learn about the manifold dimensions of Christ's wisdom, goodness, power, and love toward all humanity who came to Him in faith with their needs.

☑ **YES, I want to receive Rick Renner's monthly teaching letter!**

Simply scan the QR code to claim this resource or go to:
renner.org/claim-your-free-offer

Connect

WITH US!

www.ingramcontent.com/pod-product-compliance
Lightning Source LLC
Chambersburg PA
CBHW071642040426
42452CB00009B/1730